GCSE

COMBINED SCIENCE

Physics

Revision Guide

INTRODUCTION

This book has been specially written as a quick revision guide for students who want to succeed in their GSCE Combined Science Examination. It covers the Physics subject content of the syllabus.

It contains explanations of all the key scientific words used in the examination and the application of these words to their use in the type of questions asked by the examiner.

This book should be used with the other Combined Science revision guide books that cover the Biology and Chemistry content of the Combined Science Syllabus.

Chris Prescott

CONTENTS

1. ENERGY

Glossary

Biomass Fuel   Plant material that can be used directly as a fuel or indirectly from the gas given off (biogas which is mainly methane gas) as it decomposes.

Conduction   The way heat energy (thermal energy) is transferred through solids, and to a much lesser extent through liquids and gases.

Convection   The way in which heat energy (thermal energy) is transferred through liquids and gases by movement of the particles in the liquid or gas.

Energy   In physics terms this is the capacity of a system to do work. When work is done on or by an object, the object gains or loses energy. There are many different forms of energy like heat, kinetic, potential etc.

Evaporation   The process of a liquid changing into a gas at temperatures below its boiling point. Evaporation only occurs on the surface of a liquid when a particle has sufficient energy to escape.

Fluid   Describes a state of matter that moves by itself therefore gases, liquids and molten solids are fluids.

Fossil Fuel   Fuels formed from the remains of ancient buried organisms. These include coal, petroleum (crude oil) and natural gas.

Geothermal Energy   This is the heat energy from hot rock deep in the Earth's crust. This heat can be used to warm water or make steam for driving turbines to generate electricity.

Heat Energy   This is the energy that flows from one place to another as a result of a difference in temperature.

Hydroelectricity   Electricity produced by trapping rainwater at a high level and then allowing it to flow through electrical turbines at a lower level.

Joule   The SI unit of both work and energy. One joule is the work done by a force of one newton moving one metre in the direction of the force.

Kinetic Energy   The energy possessed by an object or particle because it is moving. The faster it moves the greater its kinetic energy.

Potential Energy   The energy stored in a body or system because of its position (gravitational potential energy), shape (elastic potential energy), nature (chemical potential energy) or state (vapours cooling down).

Power   The rate at which work is done or energy is transferred.

Radiation   General electromagnetic waves (types of light) and radioactivity.

Sankey Diagram   Energy transfer diagram with arrows of different thicknesses to indicate amount of energy being transferred.

Solar Cell (Photocell)   Device that is used to change solar energy (sunlight) into electrical energy.

Solar Power   Energy from the Sun trapped by solar panels for heating or solar cells for electricity.

Work   Energy transfer that occurs when a force causes an object to move a certain distance in the direction of the force. Work has the same unit of measurement (joule) as energy.

Key Facts

- Most of the *energy* the world uses is obtained from *fossil fuels* like coal, petroleum (crude oil) and natural gas. However once these fuels have been in use they cannot be replaced. They are *non-renewable* energy sources and are a common source of *air pollution*. It is predicted the world will run out of petroleum and natural gas by 2050. It has therefore become important to find alternative renewable energy sources which are pollution-free.

- Alternative energy sources to fossil fuels are the following *renewable energy resources* which are also *pollution-free*:

    ✓ *Solar power* traps the Sun's energy using *solar panels* to heat water. Also *solar cells* (*photocells*) are used to convert the Sun's energy into electricity. The cost of installing solar panels can be expensive. Another disadvantage of solar power is the weather and night-time limits how effective solar power can be.

- ✓ *Hydroelectric power* is when electricity is produced by trapping rainwater at a high level and then allowing it to flow through electricity turbines at a lower level. Often dams are used to store the water at high level. Also when demand for electricity is low electricity can be used to pump water back up to the high dam for use in times of high demand.

- ✓ *Tidal power* uses tidal estuaries to trap water at high tide, which is then allowed to flow through turbines which drive generators to produced electricity.

- ✓ *Wave power* uses the movement of the waves to rock large floats backwards and forwards. This movement can then be used to drive a generator to produce electricity.

- ✓ *Wind power* is the use of the Earth's atmosphere (wind) to drive generators to produce electricity. The wind has been used as a source of power in windmills, sailing ships, etc. since early times.

✓ **Geothermal power** is obtained using the heat from hot rock deep in the Earth's crust. Geothermal energy can be used to heat water in homes, or to make steam for driving turbines to generate electricity.

- **Biogas** is released when organic material (plant material, animal excrement etc.) decomposes in the absence of air. Biogas is approximately 50% methane gas and is a useful fuel for heating, cooking and lighting. Most sewage plants and many landfill sites are now designed to collect biogas. This gas is given off when sewage sludge, or buried landfill, decays anaerobically underground. Like **fossil fuels** biogas fuel produces pollutants on burning, The main **pollutant** is **carbon dioxide gas** which is a **greenhouse gas** and contributes towards **global warming.**

- Energy that flows from high temperature to low temperature is called **thermal energy**. There are four ways thermal energy can be transferred.

    1. **Conduction**
    2. **Convection**
    3. **Radiation**
    4. **Evaporation**

- **_Conduction_** is the way in which thermal energy (heat) is transferred through **_solids_** (and to a much lesser extent in liquids and gases). Materials which allow thermal energy to pass through easily are called **_conductors_** (high thermal conductivity). Those that do not are called **_insulators_**. Metals are good conductors as they have lots of free electrons and their particles (atoms) are close together. When a metal is heated, the free electrons gain kinetic energy and move more quickly in all directions moving the heat around. Conduction cannot occur if there are no particles present, so a vacuum is the perfect insulator.

- **_Convection_** is the way thermal energy (heat) is transferred through **_liquids_** and **_gases_** by movement of the particles because these materials flow (they are called fluids). When a fluid is heated, kinetic energy is transferred to its particles causing them to move faster and further apart. The fluid expands and becomes less dense than the unheated fluid. The less dense warmer fluid will rise above the more dense, colder fluid, causing the fluid to circulate. This circulating movement of a heated fluid is called a **_convection current_**.

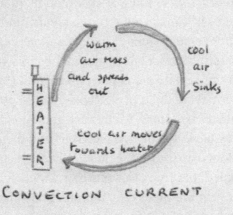

Warm air rises and spreads out

cool air Sinks

cool air moves towards heater

CONVECTION CURRENT

- ***Convection currents*** cannot take place if there are no particles (vacuum) and are reduced if the fluid's movement is restricted. Insulators like plastic fibre / fibreglass are often placed inside wall or loft cavities to prevent air from circulating and thereby preventing heat loss.

- ***Radiation*** is a general term applied to anything that travels outward from its source but which cannot be identified as a type of matter like a solid, liquid or gas. Radiation does not need particles of matter so can travel through a vacuum. It applies to ***forms of energy like heat***.

11

- ***Infrared radiation*** (***radiant heat / thermal radiation***) is taken in and given out by all objects. This radiation is the heat energy from the Sun which travels to Earth through space as radiant heat. Such heat is an electromagnetic wave mainly in the infrared region of the electromagnetic spectrum (see page 68). When the wave falls on an object the particles gain thermal energy and the temperature of the object increases. The amount of this type of radiation given out or taken in by an object depends on its temperature and its surface. The hotter the object the more infrared radiation given off.

Type of surface	*As an emitter of radiation*	*As an absorber of radiation*	*Examples*
Bright and shiny	Poor	Poor	Shiny silver paint on outside of fuel tanks
Dull (matt) and black	Good	Good	Dark clothes absorb more heat

- ***Evaporation of a liquid causes cooling*** as heat energy has escaped. Evaporation occurs when the more energetic particles on the surface of a liquid escape. This leaves the remaining particles of lower kinetic energy and therefore lower temperature. The evaporation of sweat helps to keep the body cool in hot weather.

- ***Energy transfers*** can be summarised using ***Sankey diagrams***. Here the thickness of the arrow indicates the amount of energy involved. Consider the heat energy escaping in a typical house due to poor insulation.

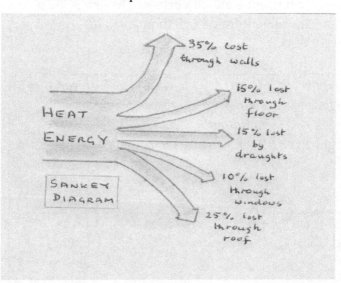

To prevent heat losses (as shown in the Sankey diagram) there is cavity wall insulation, carpets/tiling on the floor, draught excluders, double glazing and loft insulation.

- It is often necessary to work out the *energy efficiency* of different devices. The following formula can be used:

Efficiency = $\dfrac{\underline{\text{Useful energy output}}}{\text{Energy input}}$ x 100

- *Work* is done when *energy is transferred*. Energy is never lost and cannot be destroyed. Energy just changes from one form to another when work is done. Both work and energy are measured in the SI unit of *joule*.

A *joule* of work is done by a force of *1 newton* moving *1 metre* in the direction of that force.

Work is done when a force results in movement. It can be calculated using the following formula.

14

Work done = Force x ***Distance moved***

$$W = F \text{ x } s$$

W = Work done in joules (J)
F =   Force in newtons (N)
s =   Distance in metres (m)

Example

A cyclist cycles 250 m to school along a flat road. He exerts a force of 80 N when cycling. Calculate the work done, in kilojoules (kJ), by the cyclist.

Write down formula used	W = F x s
Substitute values for F and s	W = 80 x 250
Calculate work in joules	W = 2000 J
Calculate work in kilojoules	W = 2000/1000 = ***2 kJ***

Example

A mother does 2000 J of work pushing a pram 50 m along a road. Calculate the force she was exerting on the pram when she was pushing.

Write down formula used	F = W / s
Substitute values for W and s	F = 2000 / 50
Calculate force in newtons	F = ***40 N***

- *Power* is defined as the rate of doing work or the rate of transferring energy. Power is measured in the SI unit of *watt* (*1 kilowatt* (*kW*) = *1000 W*).

A *watt* of power is equal to *1 joule per second*.

$$Power = \frac{Work\ done}{Time\ taken} = \frac{Energy\ transfer}{Time\ taken}$$

$$P = \frac{W}{t}$$

P = Power in watt (W)
W = Work done in joules (J)
t = Time in seconds (s)

Example

A machine does 5 kilojoules of work in every 10 seconds. Calculate the power of the machine in watts.

Convert kilojoules into joules   5 kJ = 5 000 J
Write down formula used   P = W / t
Substitute values for W and t   P = 5 000 / 10
Calculate power in watts   P = *500 W*

- Stored or hidden energy is called *potential energy.* This stored energy may be because of an object's position (*gravitational potential energy*), shape (*elastic potential energy*), nature (*chemical potential energy*) or state (vapours cooling down).

- If a load is raised above ground level it has the potential to fall back down due to the pull of gravity. This is *gravitational potential energy* which can be calculated by the following formula:

17

Gravitational = *Mass* x *Gravitational* x *Height*
   potential   *field strength*
   energy

P.E. = ***m*** x ***g*** x ***h***

P.E. = Gravitational potential energy in joules (J)
m = Mass in kilograms (kg)
g = Gravitational field strength (9.8 N/kg)
h = Height in metres (m)

As a rough guide every metre a kilogram object falls to Earth 10 joules of gravitational potential energy is given away (g = 10 N/kg) and converted to other energy forms like kinetic energy.

Example

An apple with a mass of 200 g was growing on the top of an apple tree which was 8 metres high. What is the gravitational potential energy of the apple? Assume g = 10 N/kg

Convert 200 g into kilograms   200 / 1000 = 0.2 kg
Write down the formula for P.E.   P.E. = m x g x h
Substitute values for m, g, and h   P.E. = 0.2 x 10 x 8
Calculate potential energy in joules   = ***16 joules***

- *Kinetic energy* is the energy possessed by an object or particle because it is moving. Kinetic energy can be calculated using the following formula.

$$\textbf{\textit{Kinetic energy}} \ = \ \textbf{\textit{½ Mass}} \ \ \textit{x} \ \ \textbf{\textit{Velocity}}^2$$
$$\textbf{\textit{K.E.}} \ = \ \textbf{\textit{½ m}} \ \ \textit{x} \ \ \textbf{\textit{v}}^2$$

K.E. = Kinetic energy in joules (J)
m   = Mass in kilograms (kg)
v   = Velocity in metres per second (m/s)

Example

An apple of mass 200 g fell from the top of an 8 metre apple tree. Assuming all its gravitational potential energy was converted into kinetic energy determine the velocity of the apple just before it touched the ground. Assume g = 10 N/kg

From the previous example the gravitational potential energy of the apple at the top of the tree was 16 joules, which is the value of its kinetic energy before landing. Write down the formula for K.E.   K.E. = ½ m x v^2
Substitute values for K.E. and mass (in kilograms)

$$16 \ = \ ½ \ \ x \ \ 0.2 \ \ x \ \ v^2$$
$$v^2 = \ \ 16 / 0.1 \ = \ 160$$
$$v = \ \ \sqrt{160} \ \ = \ \textbf{\textit{12.65 m/s}}$$

2. ELECTRICITY

Glossary

Alternating Current (*a.c.*)   An electric current which reverses its direction of flow in periodic cycles. In Britain, mains electricity alternates at 50 cycles per second (frequency of 50 Hz).

Ammeter   Instrument used to measure the amount of electric current in amperes flowing through a particular point in an electrical circuit.

Battery   Number of electric cells connected together.

Coulomb   Quantity of electric charge transported by an electric current. One coulomb is equivalent to 1 amp flowing for 1 second.

Direct Current (*d.c.*)   An electric current which is flowing in one direction. All battery-operated devices use direct current.

Electric Charge   Quantity of electricity measured in coulombs.

Electric Current   Flow of electric charge (electrons) through a conductor.

Electrical Power   This indicates how many joules of energy are supplied per second. Electrical power is measured in watts / kilowatts.

Electrical Resistance   The ability of a conductor to resist, or oppose the flow of an electric current through it. Resistance is measured in ohms.

Electricity   Flow of charged particles (electrons or ions). Electricity flows around an electrical circuit as an electric current.

Electrolysis   Passing electric current though a liquid which contains ions. The liquid undergoes chemical decomposition.

Fuse   Short, thin piece of wire which overheats and melts to break the electrical circuit if more than a certain value of current flows through.

Potential Difference (p.d.)   The difference in potential of two charged points. It is measured in volts.

Static   The accumulation of electric charge on an object which is a poor conductor of electricity.

Volt   Unit of potential difference. One volt is equivalent to 1 joule of electrical energy carrying a charge of 1 coulomb.

Voltage   The potential difference or a measured value of this in volts.

Voltmeter   Instrument used to measure the potential difference (voltage) between two points in an electrical circuit.

Key Facts

- *Electricity* is a *flow of electric current* which is actually a *flow of electrons*. Electricity is a way of transferring energy which can then be *changed into various energy* forms:

    - ✓ Heat …. heating element of a fire
    - ✓ Light …. electric light bulb
    - ✓ Magnetism ….   electromagnets
    - ✓ Kinetic ….   electric motors
    - ✓ Chemical ….   electrolysis of liquids

- Simple *electrical circuits* are drawn using circuit symbols as shown in the diagrams. There are two types of circuit *series* and *parallel*.

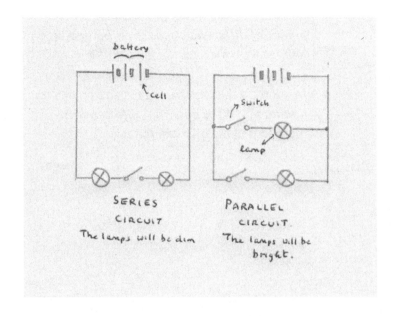

In a series circuit there is only one route round the circuit, whereas with a parallel circuit there are at least two routes. In the parallel circuit the battery can push the electricity two alternative paths so more charge can flow. As a result the *lamps* in a *parallel circuit* are *brighter* than the lamps in a series circuit.

- ***Charge*** is the ***quantity of electricity*** that is passing through the circuit. As charge flows around the circuit it transfers energy to the components. The amount of energy that a charge transfers between two point is called the ***potential difference (p.d)***. This is measured in ***volts*** and is often refered to as ***voltage***.

- In a circuit the ***current*** is measured using an ***ammeter*** and the ***potential difference*** is measured using a ***voltmeter***.

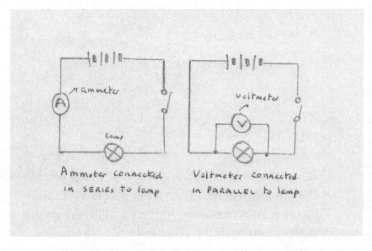

The ***ammeter*** must be ***connected in series*** to the device (lamp) it is measuring the current passing through, the ***voltmeter connected in parallel***.

- The **ammeter** measures current in units called **ampere** (**amp**, **A**). In the diagrams below the bulbs through which the current is passing are identical.

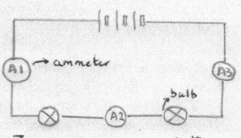

In this series circuit the current is the same throughout. Therefore the readings of ammeters A1 = A2 = A3.

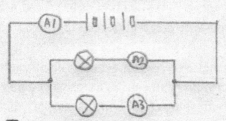

In this parallel circuit the current is split between the two branches so A1 = A2 + A3

- A *battery* produces an electric current which is flowing in one direction. This is known as a *direct current* (*d.c.*). An electric current which reverses its direction of flow in periodic cycles is called an *alternating current* (*a.c.*). In Britain, *mains electricity* alternates at 50 cycles per second (frequency of 50 Hz).

- *Static* is the accumulation of electric charge on an object which is a poor conductor of electricity. When *insulators,* like plastics, are rubbed together electrons on the surface of one insulator are transferred to the surface of the other insulator. The surface that gains electrons becomes negatively charged with static. The surface that loses electrons becomes positively charged. As the charges are fixed it is referred to as *static electricity*.

- Friction between water molecules and air currents can cause clouds to become charged with static. *Lightning* is caused when *static electricity* passes from a charged cloud to the ground. Lightning can also be between negative charged areas of cloud to positive charged areas of cloud. Static gives shocks in everyday situations like walking on carpets, combing your hair, getting out of a car etc.

- *Conductors* are substances that allow an electric current to flow through. Metals are good conductors because of their structure. Metal ions are surrounded by a 'sea' of electrons. When a potential difference is applied these electrons become mobile and carry the electricity around. *Insulators* like plastics, wood, gases and most liquids do not allow electric current to pass through as they do not have any free, mobile electrons.

- Some *conductors* allow electrons (electricity) to pass through more easily than others. These conductors have a lower *resistance (R)* . Factors that determine resistance are type of material and the thickness and length of material / wire. Thicker wire has a lower resistance and longer length of wire has a greater resistance.

- The relationship between voltage, current and resistance is given by *Ohm's law*.

Voltage = *Current* x *Resistance*

V = I x R

Voltage is measured in *volts* (*V*), *current* in *amps* (*A*) and *resistance* in *ohms* (*Ω*).

Example

Calculate the voltage necessary to send 10 milliamps of current through a 5 ohms resistor.

Convert 10 milliamps into amps   1 mA = 0.001 A

                                     10 mA = 0.010 A

Write down Ohm's law equation. $V = I \times R$

Substitute the values of I and R $V = 0.01 \times 5$

                                            $= \textbf{\textit{0.05 V}}$

Example

Calculate the resistance of a heater element if a current of 8 A passes through if connected to a 240 V supply.

Write down Ohm's law in terms of R. $R = V/I$

Substitute values for V and I. $R = 240 / 8$

                                   $= \textbf{\textit{30}}\ \Omega$

- The *resistance* of most conductors increases if the conductor becomes hot. This happens in *filament bulbs* as the filament becomes hotter the metal ions vibrate more and this restricts the movement of the mobile electrons.

Ohmic resistors e.g. carbon resistors do not get hot and obey Ohm's law, as shown by a straight-line graph of voltage against current. Filament bulbs are non-ohmic as they become hot.

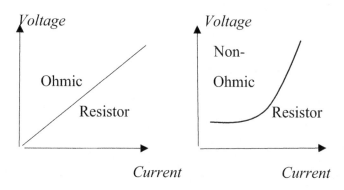

- *Electrical power* rating indicates how many joules of energy are supplied each second. Power is measured in watts and is determined by the potential difference (voltage) and current in the electrical circuit.

The electrical *power* of *1 watt* is equal to *1 joule of energy* being supplied *each second*.

- The relationship between electrical power (P) and voltage (V) and current (I) is:

Power = *Voltage* x *Current*

P = V x I

Power is measured in *watts* (*W*), *voltage* in *volts* (*V*) and *current* in *amps* (*A*).

Example

An electric fire has a power rating of 2kW. What current would flow through the fire if it is connected to a 240 V mains supply?

Convert power rating to watts	2kW	= 2000 W
Write down the formula used	I	= P / V
Substitute values for P and V	I	= 2000/ 240
		= *8.33 A*

- A *fuse* is a short, thin piece of wire which overheats and melts to break the electrical circuit if more than a certain value of current flows through. Fuses, like switches, are always placed on the live wire. All three-pin plugs are fused.

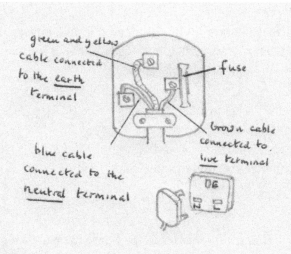

green and yellow cable connected to the earth terminal

fuse

brown cable connected to live terminal

blue cable connected to the neutral terminal

In three-pin plugs the fuse fits between the live brown wire and the pin. The **brown live wire** and the **blue neutral wire** carry the current. The **green and yellow stripped earth wire** is needed to make metal appliances safe.

Electrical device	Power (W)	Fuse rating
Cooker	8,000 W	30 A
Immersion heater	3,000 W	13 A
Iron	800 W	5 A
Colour TV	120 W	3 A
Table lamp	15 W	3 A

- *Electricity meters* in the home measure the
  amount of *electrical energy* used in *kilowatt-
  hours (kWh)*. One kilowatt hour is the amount of
  energy transferred by a 1 kW device in 1 hour.

Example

Its winter and a 1.5 kW electric fire is left on in a room for 6 hours during the day to keep it warm. The day-time rate for the electricity is 15 pence per kWh. Calculate the cost of using the fire in daytime to keep the room warm.

Write down the formula used
    Energy (kWh) = Power (kW) x Time (h)
Substitute values for power and time
    Energy = 1.5 x 6 = 9 kWh
    Cost   =   kWh x 15 p = 9 x 15p = 135p
                        = *£1.35p*

3. *MAGNETISM*
&
ELECTROMAGNETISM

Glossary

Alternating Current (*a.c.*)   An electric current which reverses its direction of flow in periodic cycles.

Commutator   Device used in d.c. electric motor to reverse the current direction every half-turn.

Direct Current (*d.c.*)   An electric current which is flowing in one direction. All battery-operated devices use direct current.

Dynamo   Generator which produces electrical energy in the form of direct current.

Electromagnet   A solenoid with a core of ferromagnetic material such as soft iron.

Electromagnetic Induction   The creation of electricity by changing the magnetic field around a wire.

Electromagnetism   When an electric current flows through a wire it creates a magnetic field around the wire.

Generator   Device that produces electrical energy

National Grid   Arrangement which transmits electricity around the country.

Relay (Electrical relay) Device which uses a small current in the coil of an electromagnet to switch on a larger current in another independent circuit. It acts as an electromagnetic switch.

Solenoid Long cylindrical coil of insulated wire. A current flowing through a solenoid produces a magnetic field which is similar to that produced by a bar magnet.

Transformer Device for changing the voltage of an alternating current without changing its frequency.

Turbine Machine or motor that is driven by a rotor or wheel that is turned around by a flow of water or gas.

Key Facts

- Simple **bar magnets** have a **N-pole**, which is attracted to the Earth's magnetic North Pole. Also at the other end of the bar magnet is the south- seeking pole or **S-pole**.

- **Magnetic fields** around magnets can be identified with **plotting compasses**. These can plot the **magnetic lines of force**. These lines never cross and the closer the line of force the stronger the magnetic field.

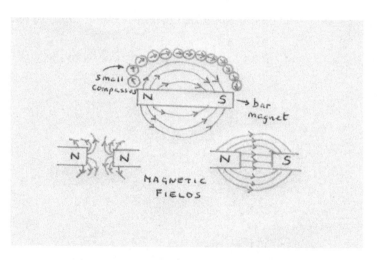

- The **rule of magnetism** is that **opposite poles attract, like poles repel**.

- Only certain metals are magnetic and therefore attracted to magnets. The three **magnetic metals** are **iron**, **cobalt** and **nickel** (and their alloys like steel etc.).

- When an electric current flows through a wire it creates a magnetic field around the wire. This is called **electromagnetism**. The strength of the magnetic field can be made stronger if the wire is wrapped into a coil around a piece of magnetic material such as iron. The strength of the magnetic field can be increase by:

  ✓ increasing the current flowing through the wire
  ✓ increasing the number of coils in the wire

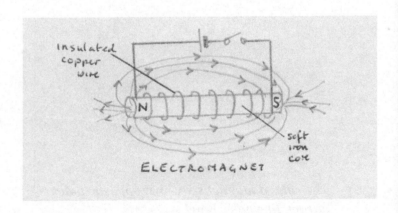

insulated copper wire

soft iron core

ELECTROMAGNET

- A *relay* is an *electromagnetic switch*. It uses a small current in the coil of an electromagnet to switch on a large current in another independent circuit.

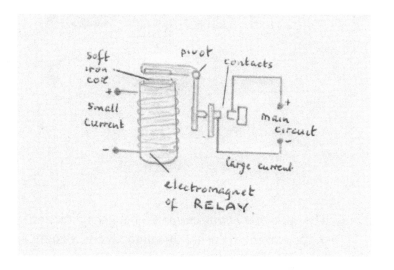

- An *electric motor* is a device which uses the motor effect to *change electrical energy into kinetic energy*. A simple direct current (d.c.) motor consists of a flat coil of current-carrying wire placed in a magnetic field. One side of the coil experiences an upward force, and the other side a downward force, so the coil rotates to produce kinetic (mechanical) energy.

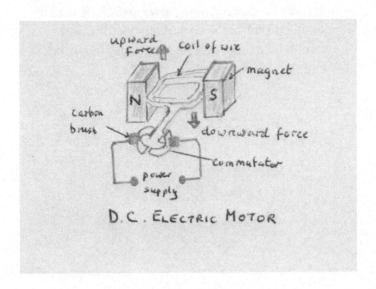

D.C. ELECTRIC MOTOR

The split-ring *commutator* changes the direction of the current to ensure the motor keeps rotating.

- *Electricity* can be *generated* by changing the magnetic field around a wire. This is called *electromagnetic induction*.

- A *dynamo* exhibits electromagnetic induction and converts *kinetic energy into electrical energy* by rotating conducting coils in a magnetic field. In general terms a dynamo is a generator but as it has a split-ring commutator it produces a direct current so is a *d.c. generator*.

41

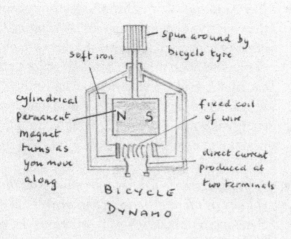

Labels on diagram:
- spun around by bicycle tyre
- soft iron
- cylindrical permanent magnet turns as you move along
- N S
- fixed coil of wire
- direct current produced at two terminals

BICYCLE DYNAMO

- **Power stations** produce electricity on a large scale. Unlike dynamos power stations produce alternating current so are **a.c. generators**. Inside a power station the following changes occur:

  - ➤ **Fuel** is burnt to **heat water** and produce **steam**
  - ➤ High pressured **steam drives a turbine**
  - ➤ The **rotary motion** of the turbine causes magnets to turn **inducing electricity in generators.**

- The *National Grid* transmits electricity around the country. The grid supplies *alternating current* because it uses transformers which only work with alternating current. To reduce power loss in the grid the electricity is transmitted at very high voltage (low current), so that less energy is wasted as heat, as a high current would heat the transmission wire.

- A *transformer* is a device for *changing the voltage of an alternating current* without changing its frequency. If it *increases* the *voltage* it is called a *step-up-transformer*, if it *decreases* the *voltage* it is called a *step-down-transformer*.

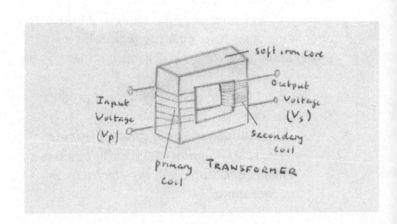

- A *transformer* consists of *two coils of wire* wound on the same soft-iron core. The alternating current in the primary coil causes an alternating magnetic field in the iron core. This induces an alternating current in the secondary coil. The two coils are not connected and the *power* (voltage x current) in *each coil* is the *same*.

primary x *primary* = *secondary* x *secondary*
voltage (V_p) *current (I_p)* *voltage (V_s)* *current (I_s)*

- If there are *more turns on the secondary coil* than on the primary coil then the voltage will be stepped up (current reduced). This is called a *step-up transformer*. If there are *less turns on the secondary coil* than on the primary coil then the voltage will be stepped down (current increased). This is called a *step-down transformer*.

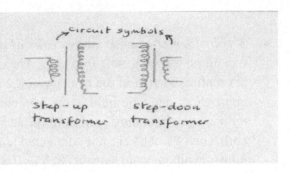

circuit symbols

step - up
transformer

step - down
transformer

primary coil voltage (V_p) =
secondary coil voltage (V_s)

> ***number of primary turns (N_p)***
> ***number of secondary turns (N_s)***

Example

Calculate the output voltage (secondary coil) from a transformer when the input voltage (primary coil) is 240 V, the number of turns on the primary coil is 400 turns and on the secondary coil is 20 turns.

Write down the formula used $\dfrac{V_p}{V_s} = \dfrac{N_p}{N_s}$

Substitute known values $\dfrac{240}{V_s} = \dfrac{400}{20}$

$$V_s = \frac{240 \times 20}{400} = \textit{12 V}$$

---

4. FORCES
&
MOTION

Glossary

Acceleration   The rate of change of increasing velocity (or speed). Acceleration, like velocity, is a vector quantity as it has both size and direction.

Force   Pushing or pulling action which can change the shape of an object, or make a stationary object move or make a moving object change its speed or direction. Forces are a vector quantity as they have direction.

Mass   This is quantity of matter normally measured in grams or kilograms.

Scalar Quantity   This is a quantity that has magnitude (size), but not direction. Examples of scalar quantities are energy, mass, density etc.

Speed   The rate at which an object moves expressed as distance travelled in a certain time. Speed is a scalar quantity as it has magnitude (size) but no direction.

Vector Quantity   This is a quantity which has both magnitude (size) and direction. Examples of vector quantities are displacement, velocity, acceleration, force etc.

Velocity   The rate at which an object moves in a particular direction expressed as distance travelled in a certain time. Velocity is a vector quantity as it has size and direction.

Key Facts

- The *speed* of an object is the same size as the *velocity* of that object. The only difference is speed does not have any specific direction (is a *scalar quantity*), velocity does have a specific direction (*vector quantity*). Both speed and velocity can be calculated from the following equation:

$$\text{Speed } (v) = \frac{\text{Distance } (s)}{\text{Time } (t)}$$

Example

A car travels up the motorway at a constant speed. It covers 6 kilometres in 5 minutes. What is its speed in metres / second?

Convert distance and time into metres and seconds.

  6 km = 6000 m 5 min = 5 x 60 = 300 s

Write down the formula used v = s / t

Substitute values for distance and time

    v = 6000 / 300 = *20 m/s*

- Acceleration is a measure of how speed or velocity changes with time. It can be calculated from the following equation:

$$Acceleration\ (a)\ =\ \frac{Change\ in\ speed\ (v\text{-}u)}{Time\ taken\ (t)}$$

$$a\ =\ \frac{v\text{-}u}{t} \quad \text{where } v = \textit{final speed}$$
$$u = \textit{initial speed}$$

Initial and final speeds are measured in metres per second (m/s). Acceleration is measured in metres per second per second (m/s/s).

Example

A motorcyclist accelerated from 5 m/s to 40 m/s in 8 seconds. Calculate the acceleration of the motorcyclist.

Write down the formula used   a = v-u / t
Substitute values for initial and final speeds and time
$$a = \ 40\text{-}5\ /\ 8 = 35/8 = \textit{4.375 m/s/s}$$

- A ***distance-time graph*** is a good way to summarize journeys and give information about speed and acceleration.

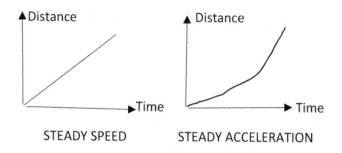

STEADY SPEED   STEADY ACCELERATION

- A ***speed-time graph*** provides information about speed and acceleration. The area under the graph also gives information about distance travelled.

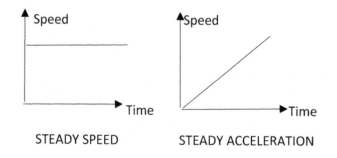

STEADY SPEED   STEADY ACCELERATION

Example

Use the following speed-time graph of a car to calculate the total distance travelled.

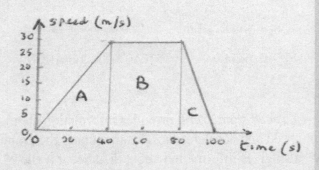

The total distance travelled is given by the area under the graph.

Area A = ½ x 40 x 30 = 600 m

Area B = 40 x 30 = 1200 m

Area C = ½ x 20 x 30 = 300 m

Total distance travelled = 600 + 1200 + 300

= *2100 m = 2.1 km*

- The acceleration of a particular object depends on the mass of the object and the force which is applied to it. The relevant formula is:

Force (*F*) = *Mass* (*m*) x *Acceleration* (*a*)

$$\frac{F}{m \times a}$$

- *Force* is measured in *newtons* (*N*), *mass* in *kilograms* (*kg*) and *acceleration* in *metres per second per second* (*m/s/s*).

Example 1

What is the force which a catapult exerts on a 250 g stone which leaves the catapult with an acceleration of 10 m/s/s.

Convert mass into kilograms   250/1000 = 0.25 kg
Write down formula you are using   F = m x a
Substitute the values of m and a   F = 0.25 x 10
                                                      = *2.5 N*

Example 2

Calculate the acceleration on a car of mass 600 kg with a resulting forward force of 8000 N.

Write down the formula you are using   a = F/m
Substitute the values of F and m   a = 8000 / 600
                                    = *13.33 m/s/s*

Example 3

A football is kicked with a force of 20 N which produces an acceleration of 15 m/s/s. What is the mass of the football?

Write down the formula you are using   m = F/a
Substitute the values of F and a   m = 20 / 15
                                    = *1.33 kg*

- When a driver stops a vehicle the *stopping distance* is made up of a *thinking distance* (the distance travelled in the time it takes the driver to react) and the *braking distance* (the distance travelled in the time it takes from beginning to brake until the vehicle stops).

$$\begin{array}{ccccc} \textit{Stopping} & = & \textit{Thinking} & + & \textit{Braking} \\ \textit{Distance} & & \textit{Distance} & & \textit{Distance} \end{array}$$

- **Thinking distance** can be affected by the following:

  - ✓ Faster speed further travel when thinking
  - ✓ Tiredness of individual who is driving
  - ✓ Level of concentration of driver
  - ✓ Medication or drugs used by driver
  - ✓ If the driver has been drinking alcohol

- **Breaking distance** can be affected by the following:

  - ✓ Faster speed further travel before stopping
  - ✓ Condition of brakes on the vehicle
  - ✓ Condition of tyres on the vehicle
  - ✓ Size and mass of vehicle
  - ✓ Condition of road surface

5. WAVES

Glossary

Amplitude   The height of a wave from its peak to its mean rest position. The size of the amplitude indicates the energy carried by the wave.

Angle of Incidence   Angle between the incident ray and the normal ray when a light ray is reflected.

Angle of Reflection   Angle between the reflected ray and the normal ray when a light ray is reflected.

Critical Angle   This is the smallest angle of incidence at which total internal reflection can occur.

Compression   Squashing together of particles in a medium as a longitudinal wave (like sound) passes through.

Decibel (dB)   Unit of sound intensity or loudness.

Diffraction   The spreading or bending of waves which occurs when a wave goes around an obstacle or through a gap.

Echolocation   Method of using the reflection of sound waves off an object to determine its exact position.

Electromagnetic Spectrum   Family of transverse waves including ultraviolet, visible light, infrared etc.

Focal Length   Distance between the optical centre of a lens and its focal point.

Focal Point (*F*)   Point through which all rays travelling parallel to the principal axis pass after refraction through a lens.

Frequency   The frequency of a wave is the number of oscillations per second. Frequency is measured in hertz (Hz).

Hertz (*Hz*)   The SI unit of frequency of waves equal to one cycle / oscillation per second.

Incident Ray   This is the light ray before reflection on a surface.

Longitudinal Wave   This is one in which the oscillation or vibration is along the line of the direction in which the wave is travelling. Sound is a longitudinal wave.

Medium   Substance through which a wave travels. Air and glass are examples of a medium.

Normal Ray   Imaginary line at right angles to a surface where a light ray strikes it.

Pitch   Property of sound determined by its frequency. High-pitched sounds have high frequencies.

Principal Axis (Optical Axis)   Imaginary line which passes through the optical centre at right angles to the lens.

Progressive Wave   This is one that transports energy (but not matter) away from a source. Sound and light are progressive waves.

Rarefaction   Spreading apart of particles in a medium as a longitudinal wave (like sound) passes through.

Reflected ray   This is the light ray after reflection off a surface.

Reflection   The bouncing off of a wave from a surface / barrier. Only the direction of the wave changes. Reflection occurs with sound waves, light waves and other electromagnetic waves.

Refraction   The change in direction of a wave as it passes from one medium to another. During refraction there is a change in speed, direction and wavelength, but not in frequency.

Seismic Wave   Shock wave of an earthquake. There are three types: p-waves, s-waves and l-waves.

Sonar   ***So***und ***na***vigation and ***r***anging is a system which uses ultrasound for echolocation to detect underwater objects.

Total Internal Reflection   This occurs with a light ray when the angle of incidence exceeds a certain value, the ray is reflected internally rather than being refracted.

Transverse wave   This is a type of wave in which the oscillation or vibration is at right angles to the line of the direction in which the wave is travelling. Light is a transverse wave.

Ultrasound   Sound above the human hearing range (above approximately 20 000 Hz).

Wavelength   This is the distance between two identical points on a wave e.g. two adjacent peaks or two adjacent troughs.

Key Facts

- There are two types of wave: ***longitudinal wave*** and ***transverse wave***.

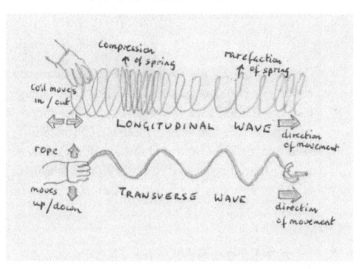

- ***Sound*** is an example of a ***longitudinal wave***. Sound is produced when objects oscillate (vibrate backwards and forwards). As the oscillating objects moves forward, it squashes the particles in the medium together (***compression***). When the object moves backwards, the particles in the medium become widely spaced (***rarefaction***). ***Vibration*** occurs in the ***same direction as the wave is travelling***. Sound ***requires a medium***, like air, to travel through.

- *Light* and other *electromagnetic waves* are examples of *transverse waves*. This time the oscillation or vibration is at right angles to the direction of movement. Such waves *do not require a medium* to pass through (travel through a vacuum).

- All *longitudinal waves* and *transverse waves* are called *progressive waves* as they transport energy (but not matter) away from a source. The speed of these waves varies enormously. The speed of sound in air (330 m/s) is about a million times slower than the speed of light (300 000 000 m/s), which is why you see lightning before you hear thunder.

- All waves have certain characteristics.

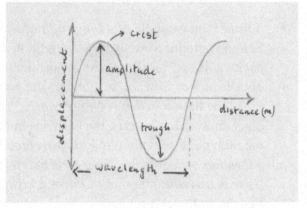

- ✓ They ***transport energy*** without moving any material or matter along.
- ✓ They have a specific ***frequency***. This is the number of oscillations (complete waves / repeating patterns) which pass a point each second.
- ✓ They have a specific ***amplitude***. This is the maximum displacement from peak to mean rest position.
- ✓ They have a specific ***wavelength***. This is the distance between two identical points on a wave.
- ✓ They have a ***repeating shape***.

- The velocity (speed) of a wave in a given medium is constant. The relationship between velocity and frequency and wavelength is:

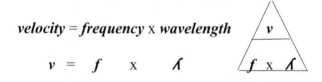

velocity = frequency x ***wavelength***

v = f x $\wedge$

Wave velocity is measured in metres per second (m/s), frequency in hertz (Hz) (oscillations per second) and wavelength in metres (m).

Example

A loudspeaker produces sound waves with a frequency of 0.5 kHz (kilohertz). The waves have a wavelength of 0.66 m. Calculate the speed of the sound waves.

Convert frequency into hertz 0.5 kHz x1000 = 500 Hz

Write down formula used $v = f \times \lambda$

Substitute values for f and λ $v = 500 \times 0.66$

Calculate speed $v = \textbf{\textit{330 m/s}}$

Example

A radio station broadcasts on a wavelength of 300 m. The speed of the radio waves is 3×10^8 m/s. Calculate the frequency of the radio broadcast in kilohertz.

Speed is 3×10^8 m/s = 300 000 000 m/s

Write down formula used $f = v / \lambda$

Substitute values for v and λ $f = 300\ 000\ 000 / 300$

Calculate frequency $f = 1\ 000\ 000$ Hz
                             $= 1\ 000$ kHz

- ***Reflection*** of a wave occurs when a wave hits a surface and bounces off. Mirrors are commonly used for regular reflection of light rays.

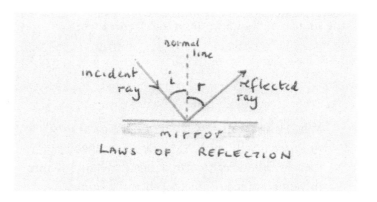

There are ***two laws of reflection***:

1. The ***incident ray***, ***reflected ray*** and ***normal ray*** (imaginary line at right angles to the surface where the light ray strikes) ***are all in the same plane***.

2. The ***angle of incidence*** (***i***) (angle between incident ray and normal ray) is ***equal to the angle of reflection*** (***r***) (angle between normal and reflected ray).

64

Type of mirror	Type of image	Uses
Plane	same size as object	wall mirror / wardrobe mirror
Concave	magnified when close to mirror	shaving / make up mirror
Convex	smaller than the object	car's wing mirror

- When a *wave* moves from *one medium into another* it will either slow down or speed up. This is called *refraction*. Consider light passing through a piece of glass. When the light wave enters the glass, it slows down as its wavelength gets smaller. On leaving the glass it speeds up as its wavelength gets larger. If the light wave enters the glass at an angle, then the wavefront also changes direction as the wave slows down. *Lens* are commonly used for refraction of light.

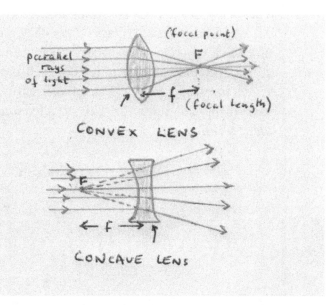

CONVEX LENS

CONCAVE LENS

- A *convex lens* causes *parallel rays of light* to *converge to a focal point* of the lens.

- A *concave lens* causes *parallel rays of light* to *diverge* as if they were *coming from the focal point* of the lens.

- When a ray of light passes from a dense medium to a less dense medium (glass to air), they are refracted away from the normal. When the angle of incidence exceeds a certain value, called the *critical angle*, the ray is reflected internally rather than being refracted. This is called *total internal reflection*.

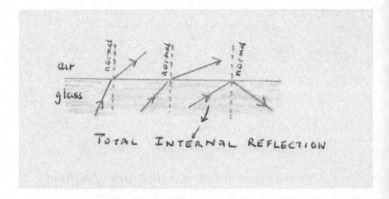

TOTAL INTERNAL REFLECTION

- *Optic fibres* use *total internal reflection* for light rays to travel along a hollow tube in the form of a cable.

- The *electromagnetic spectrum* is a family of different kinds of *transverse waves*. All the waves travel at the *same speed* in a vacuum. This is the *speed of light 300 000 000 m/s*. However different waves have different wavelengths and frequencies and this results in the different waves being used in different ways (see table below).

Type of wave	Frequency	Wavelength	Uses
Gamma rays	High	Low	killing cancer cells
X rays			looking at bones
Ultraviolet			sun-tan beds
Visible			photography
Infrared			TV remote controls
Microwaves			cooking
Radio/ TV waves	Low	High	TV / radio

68

- *Earthquakes* are sudden movement of the Earth's crust. Earthquakes produce *seismic waves.* These are made up of *longitudinal primary waves* (*P-waves*) and *transverse secondary waves* (*S-waves*). S-waves can only travel through solid rock whereas P-waves can travel through liquid and solid.

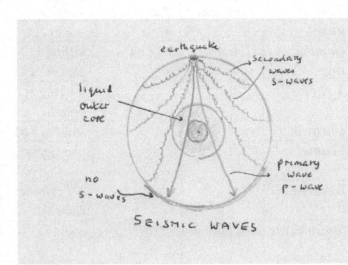

SEISMIC WAVES

- ***Sound*** is a progressive ***longitudinal wave*** caused by the vibration of an elastic medium such as air. The speed of sound depends on the density and temperature of the medium through which it is passing. ***Sound waves cannot travel through a vacuum*** because there is no material (medium) to vibrate. In general sound travels fastest in solids (5000 m/s in concrete), slower in liquids (1400 m/s in water) and slowest in gases (330 m/s in air). This is because the particles in solids are closest together, so the vibrations of the sound are passed on more rapidly.

- The ***frequency of a sound*** wave is called its ***pitch***. Sound with a frequency above the range of human hearing (above 20 000 Hz) is called ***ultrasound***. Ultrasound is used in ***sonar***.

short burst
of ultrasonic
waves travel
to the sea bed

the reflected
waves arrive
at the receiver
1.5 s later

- The *amplitude of a sound* wave is called the *loudness* of the sound and is measured in *decibels* (*dB*).

Sound (loudness)	Decibel level
threshold of hearing	0 dB
bird singing	30 dB
normal conversation	60 dB
road drill	80 dB
loud thunderclap	110 dB
threshold of pain	130 dB

- When a wave passes through a small gap the wavefronts change shape. This process is known as diffraction. Diffraction is most noticeable when the size of the gap is equivalent to the wavelength of the waves.

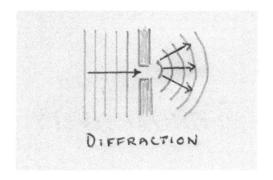

DIFFRACTION

6. RADIOACTIVITY

Glossary

Alpha Particle (*α radiation*)   This is a positively charged helium nucleus which is ejected from certain radioactive nuclei.

Atomic Number (*Proton Number*)   The number of protons in the nucleus of a particular atom of an element.

Beta radiation (*β radiation*)   High-energy emitted from certain radioactive nuclei.

Carbon Dating   Comparing the amounts of radioactive carbon-14 in dead material (like wooden artefacts, leather sandals etc.) with the levels of carbon-14 in living material.

Electron   Negatively charged particle, with very little mass, which orbits around the nucleus in atoms.

Gamma Radiation (*γ radiation*)   An electromagnetic wave of very short wavelength and high frequency emitted from certain radioactive nuclei.

Gieger-Muller tube (*Geiger Counter)*   Electronic tube which detects radioactive particles indicating the number of particles detected in the tube per second.

Half-life (*T* ½)   The time it takes for half of the atoms in a radioactive sample to undergo radioactive decay.

Isotopes   Atoms of a particular element with the same number of protons and electrons but different numbers of neutrons in their nucleus.

Mass number   The sum of the number of protons and neutrons in the nucleus of an atom of an element.

Neutron   Particle found in the nucleus of atoms which has no charge and the same mass as a proton.

Nuclear fission   Process by which a heavy, unstable nucleus is split up into two or more smaller nuclei.

Nuclear fusion   Collision and joining together of two light nuclei to form a heavier more stable nucleus. Enormous amounts of energy are released as a small amount of mass changes to energy.

Proton   Particle found in the nucleus of atoms which has a positive charge and the same mass as a neutron.

Radioactivity Decay   Spontaneous disintegration of a radioactive nucleus, giving off alpha or beta particles, often together with gamma rays.

Key Facts

- Matter is made up of atoms which have a small central nucleus (containing protons and neutrons) surrounded by shells of orbiting electrons. Some atoms are unstable and break down to form more stable nuclei. This is called ***nuclear fission***.

- When atoms decay they are said to be ***radioactive*** and emit different types of ***ionising radiation***.

   There are three possible types:

1. ***Alpha radiation*** is made up of ***alpha (α) particles*** which are positively charged, made up of ***two protons*** and ***two neutrons*** (equivalent to the helium nucleus). This type of radiation is not very penetrating and can be stopped by a sheet of paper.

2. ***Beta radiation*** is made up of ***beta (β) particles*** which are negatively charged and identical to ***electrons***. This type of radiation can be stopped by a thin sheet (2 mm) of metal.

3. **Gamma radiation** (*γ rays*) is an **electromagnetic wave** and has no charge, unlike the other two forms of radiation. This type of radiation is very penetrating and can only being stopped by thick concrete or lead.

- **Electric** and **magnetic fields** will deflect the 'heavy' alpha particles a lot and the 'lighter' beta particle a small amount. They will not deflect gamma rays.

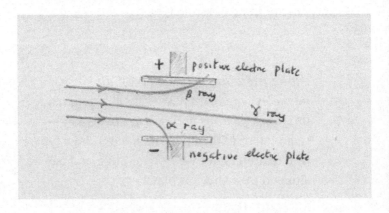

- Levels of radiation are measured using a **Geiger-Muller tube** connected to a counter. Even when there is no radioactive source being used there is still ionizing radiation present. This is called **background radiation**.

- The main sources of *background radiation* are:

  - ✓ cosmic rays from the Sun
  - ✓ radioactive gases, like radon, present in the atmosphere
  - ✓ radioactive substances, like rocks or minerals, found in the ground

- Radioactive material decays over time. The *time it takes for half of the atoms in a radioactive sample to undergo radioactive decay* is called its *half-life*. This may be hours (sodium-24), days or even thousands of years (carbon-14).

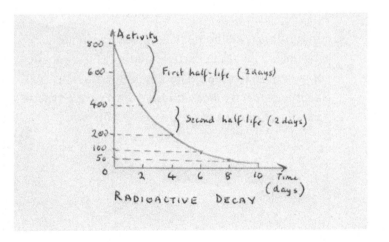

- *Nuclear equations* can be used to represent giving off a certain type of radiation. Each nucleus is represented by its *chemical symbol* and the *mass number (number of protons and neutrons)* and the *atomic number (number of protons)* are written in front of the symbol.

$$\text{\textit{mass number}} \longrightarrow 238$$
$$\text{\textit{chemical symbol}} \longrightarrow U$$
$$\text{\textit{atomic number}} \longrightarrow 92$$

In a nuclear equation the mass numbers and atomic numbers must balance on both sides of the equation.

- In *alpha decay* the nucleus gives off an alpha particle. The alpha particle given off is equivalent to a helium nucleus. The remaining nucleus (new element) has its *mass number decreased by four* and its *atomic number decreased by two*.

$$^{235}_{92}U \longrightarrow ^{231}_{90}Th + ^{4}_{2}\alpha$$

79

- In **beta decay** the nucleus gives off a beta particle. The beta particle given off is equivalent to an electron. The remaining nucleus (new element) has its **atomic number increased by one** but its **mass number remains the same**.

$$^{14}_{6}C \longrightarrow \, ^{14}_{7}N \, + \, ^{0}_{-1}\beta$$

- **Nuclear fission** is the process by which a heavy, unstable nucleus is split up into two or more smaller nuclei. Most nuclear fission occurs by firing high-energy neutrons at unstable nuclei like uranium-235 or plutonium-239. This releases **vast amounts of energy**. One kilogram of uranium-235 releases as much energy as the burning of 2 million kilograms of coal. The products of nuclear fission are normally highly radioactive and therefore need to be disposed of safely.

- **Nuclear fusion** involves the collision and joining together of two light nuclei to form a heavier more stable nucleus. It occurs at very high temperatures and releases **vast amounts of energy** as a small amount of mass changes into energy.

An example is on the *Sun* where hydrogen isotopes (deuterium and tritium) join to form the element helium. Scientists are trying to develop nuclear fusion processes on Earth that can be used to generate electrical energy.

- There are many and varied *uses of radioactivity*:

    ✓ Smoke detectors contain a source of alpha radiation. Smoke reduces the number of alpha particles so setting off the alarm.

    ✓ Beta rays are used to monitor the thickness of metal or cardboard containers.

    ✓ Gamma rays have medical uses including destroying cancer cells. They are also used to kill bacteria. They are therefore used to sterilize medical equipment and preserve food.

    ✓ Gamma rays are also used to detect leaks in underground pipes, identifying faults in welding, thickness, holes etc.

- Radioactive material can also be used in *radioactive dating*. Igneous rock can be aged as it contains small quantities of radioactive uranium-238. This has a half-life of 4500 million years and decays to form lead. Working out the ratio of lead to uranium in a sample of rock can be used to age the rock sample.

- *Radioactive carbon-14* is found in living material. This has a half-life of 5700 years and decays to carbon-12. Working out the ratio of carbon-14 to carbon-12 can be used to calculate the age of the plant or animal material. This is called *radioactive carbon dating*.

7.   THE EARTH
&
BEYOND

Glossary

Asteroid (***Minor Planet***)   Fragments of rock that orbit the Sun in a belt between the orbits of Mars and Jupiter.

Big-Bang Theory   This suggests that the universe was formed from a highly dense central mass that exploded around 15 thousand million (15 billion) years ago.

Black Hole   Region in space where gravity is so strong that even light cannot escape.

Centripetal Force   This is a force directed to the centre which causes a body to move in a circular orbit.

Comet   A lump of ice and rock orbiting the Sun in a non-circular orbit.

Galaxy   Giant collection of stars, gas and dust held together by gravitational attraction between its components.

Gravity (***Gravitational Force***)   Force of attraction objects have on one another because of their masses. The larger the mass the greater the gravitational force.

Milky Way   The galaxy to which our Sun and its planets (solar system) belong.

Nebula   Cloud of gas from which stars are formed.

Nuclear fusion   Collision and joining together of two light nuclei to form a heavier more stable nucleus. Enormous amounts of energy are released as a small amount of mass changes to energy.

Red Shift   When stars are moving away from the Earth it lengthens the wavelength of their light. This shifts the light they produce towards the red end of the spectrum, confirming the universe is expanding.

Satellite   Spacecraft or other artificial body put in orbit around a planet to collect information or transmit signals.

Solar system   Our Sun and the nine planets that orbit it.

Star   A celestial body that generates its own light and heat from nuclear fusion within its core. Our Sun is one star among billions which make up the universe.

Sunspot   Dark patch on the Sun's surface resulting from a localized fall in temperature (from 6000 °C to about 4000 °C).

Supernova   Explosive brightening of a star which results when an old a very massive star uses up most of its fuel in nuclear fusion and collapses under the force of its own gravity.

Universe All the matter, energy and space that exists. It is estimated our universe consist of around a billion (thousand million) galaxies.

White Dwarf Star This describes a medium-sized star like our Sun.

Key Facts

- The ***solar system*** is made up of the ***Sun*** and the ***eight planets*** that orbit it (Pluto is now classed as a dwarf planet).

- The ***Sun*** is the star at the ***centre of our solar system***. It is about 150 million km from Earth and has a diameter about 110 times that of Earth. The temperature inside is estimated at around 15 million ^0C and on the surface about 6000 ^0C. The core of the Sun is so hot atoms are broken down into ions and electrons (plasma). The Sun is about 75% hydrogen and 25% helium, with much less than 1% heavier elements. Light from the Sun takes about 8 minutes to reach Earth.

- The *planets* are attracted to the Sun by the force of gravity and orbit in elliptical or oval orbits.

Planet	Number of moons	Average surface temp (^0C)	Type of planet
Mercury	0	350	Small rocky planet
Venus	0	460	Small rocky planet
Earth	1	20	Small rocky planet
Mars	2	-40	Small rocky planet
Jupiter	16 +1 ring	-120	Gaseous giant
Saturn	18 - 7 rings	-180	Gaseous giant
Uranus	15 - 11 rings	-210	Gaseous giant
Neptune	8 - 4 rings	-220	Gaseous giant
Pluto	1	-230	Dwarf planet

Increasing distance from Sun

- An *asteroid* is fragments of rock that orbit the Sun in a belt between the orbits of Mars and Jupiter.

- A *comet* is a lump of ice and rock orbiting the Sun in a non-circular orbit. As a comet nears the inner part of the solar system, the Sun heats it up and produces a tail of gas. Most of the time comets cannot be seen because they are too far away from the Sun.

- A *satellite* is a spacecraft or other artificial body put in orbit around a planet (like Earth) to collect information or transmit signals. The gravitational force (weight of the satellite) provides the *centripetal force* needed to keep the satellite in a circular path around the Earth. For as satellite to stay in a particular orbit, it must travel at a certain speed. If it travels at less than this speed, it will spiral inwards towards Earth. If it travels at greater than this speed, it could escape the gravitational pull and go into space. For a satellite just above the Earth's atmosphere an orbital speed of 8 km/s allows the satellite to be in a *geostationary orbit*. This is when it appears to be stationary but is orbiting the Earth at exactly the same speed as the Earth is rotating. It therefore remains in the same position above the Earth.

88

- Our Sun is part of a group of stars called a *galaxy*. The galaxy to which our Sun and its planets (solar system) belong is called the *Milky Way* galaxy and this is made up of billions of different stars. These stars vary in size and change in form over billions of years. This is called *stellar evolution*.

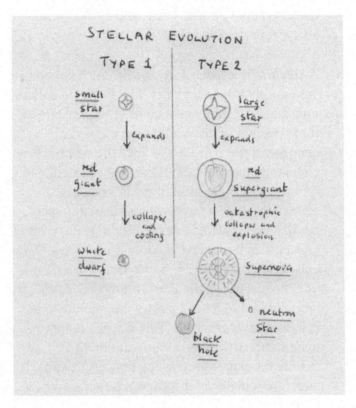

- The life-cycle of a star begins as a cloud of hydrogen gas, called a **nebula**. Gravity pulls the hydrogen atoms together and at high temperatures nuclear fusion takes place. This produces light and vast amounts of energy. The stars then expand and depending on their size produce **red giants** or red **supergiants**.
Eventually when the nuclear fusion reactions are complete the core of the star starts to collapse. Small stars form **white dwarfs** and larger stars explode to form a **supernova**. A supernova is brighter than a whole galaxy of stars but eventually over time collapse to form small and extremely dense **neutron star** or a **black hole**.
A black hole is a region in space where gravity is so strong that even light cannot escape.

- It is thought that the **Universe** was formed around 15 billion years ago and has been expanding and cooling ever since. It is estimated that it contains 10^{41} kg of mass collected into 10^9 (a billion (thousand million)) galaxies.

- Evidence for how the universe was formed is obtained by analyzing the **frequency of light** from distant galaxies. If a star is moving away from Earth the light waves that reach Earth will have a lower frequency. This shift to a lower frequency is called the *red shift*. Light from all distant galaxies shows this red shift and confirms these galaxies are moving away from the Earth. At present the *Universe is expanding*.

- The *future of the universe is uncertain*. Astronomers predict three possibilities:

  ➤ The Universe just keeps on expanding. This is because the galaxies overcome the forces of gravity acting between them.

  ➤ The Universe will start to contract. This is because the forces of gravity between the galaxies are greater than the expanding force.

  ➤ The galaxies remain in fixed positions. This is because forces of gravity become equal to the expanding forces.

APPENDIX

PHYSICS DATA SHEET

The equations that follow are normally given on Data Sheets as part of the GCSE Science (Physics) Exam Paper.

electricity: current, resistance, and potential difference

charge flow $=$ current $\times$ time

resistance in series $R_{total} = R_1 + R_2$

potential difference $=$ current $\times$ resistance

mass, force and weight

force $=$ mass x acceleration

force $=$ $\dfrac{\text{change in momentum}}{\text{time}}$

force = spring constant × extension

moment of a force = force × distance

weight = mass × gravitational field strength

pressure = $\dfrac{\text{force}}{\text{area}}$

density = $\dfrac{\text{mass}}{\text{volume}}$

energy and efficiency

kinetic energy = $0.5 \times \text{mass} \times \text{speed}^2$

elastic potential energy
$$= 0.5 \times \text{spring constant} \times \text{extension}^2$$

gravitational potential energy
$$= \text{mass} \times \text{gravitational field strength} \times \text{height}$$

change in thermal energy
$$= \text{mass} \times \text{specific heat capacity} \times \text{temperature change}$$

thermal energy for change in state
   = mass × specific latent heat

energy transferred = charge flow × potential difference

energy transferred = power × time

efficiency = $\dfrac{\text{useful output energy transfer}}{\text{total input energy transfer}}$

efficiency = $\dfrac{\text{useful power output}}{\text{total power output}}$

light and sound

wave speed = frequency × wavelength

period = $\dfrac{1}{\text{frequency}}$

magnification = $\dfrac{\text{size of image}}{\text{size of real object}}$

speed

distance travelled $=$ speed $\times$ time

$$\text{acceleration} = \frac{\text{change in velocity}}{\text{time taken}}$$

momentum $=$ mass $\times$ velocity

velocity $=$ frequency $\times$ wavelength

$(\text{final velocity})^2 - (\text{initial velocity})^2$
$= 2 \times$ acceleration $\times$ distance

work and power

work done $=$ force $\times$ distance

$$\text{power} = \frac{\text{energy transferred}}{\text{time}}$$

$$\text{power} = \frac{\text{work done}}{\text{time}}$$

power $=$ potential difference $\times$ current

power $=$ $(\text{current})^2 \times$ resistance

INDEX

Printed in Great Britain
by Amazon

40695576R00056